T0064681

Carlos
COMING
TO
AMERICA

CARLOS R. BARRON

ARCHWAY
PUBLISHING

Archway Publishing books may be ordered
through booksellers or by contacting:

Archway Publishing
1663 Liberty Drive
Bloomington, IN 47403
www.archwaypublishing.com
1 (888) 242-5904

ISBN: 978-1-4808-5700-1 (sc)
ISBN: 978-1-4808-5701-8 (e)

Library of Congress Control Number: 2018900552

Print information available on the last page.

Archway Publishing rev. date: 01/17/2018

*This book is dedicated to
my wife Yalila Barron*

I will start my book today; I live in Milwaukee, WI. Today is January **31,2001 in a very cold winter that is normal in Wisconsin. This book is mostly like a diary and events that brought me to the United States of America on September 1958. It all started when my oldest brother In Bolivia gave me a book to learn English the name of the book was "El Ingles Moderno" meaning "Modern English"; it was the best book I read, every lesson had an exercise both in grammar and understanding of the lessons. The object was to write in English translating from Spanish; in other words, there were good lessons; it took me one year to study page after page that book, which helped me with my English lessons I had in High School in the city of Oruro, Bolivia; around 1952, by the way the name of my High School was School was "Simon Bolivar", name of the liberator of many nations in South America from the Spaniards.**

So, when I was a senior I had good command of the English language that I could understand most what they said in the movies, my friend and classmate Enrique Garcia Ayaviri had the same desire like me to learn English so we tried to make friends with American or English tourists that came for Carnival to Oruro, city, Carnival is normally in the month of February.

I will always remember when Enrique and I met an American Lady, who was a reporter for Time magazine, we became her guide and translators for her; it was a nice experience that lasted two days, this was approximately in 1956. I got a Student visa after the Milwaukee School of Engineering because I was accepted after I wrote a letter of my desire to study in that School, at the time I was a student of the University of La Paz, was studying Petroleum Engineering, and MSOE did advertise about The Milwaukee School. of Engineering, eventually after I got the student visa, my trip was in September of 1958. Beside the School year in Milwaukee started on the month of September.

Did not have the money for the trip, plus I remember it costed $240 dollars per quarter, my mother sold her small house that she had in a Town called Uncia, that was the place I was born, anyway she collected $ 600 dollars, plus I took my small allowance I had from the House Patiño, like $200 dollars.

For the information of the reader Mr Patiño was a Bolivian millionaire, that made his money selling mineral especially Tin, during the second world war, Tin was the base of cans for food for the allied Army, Tin has many industrial applications, and Bolivia was the major exporter of that time.

I forgot, to mention, while we were in High School with Enrique, we were so motivated to learn English that we barrowed a dictionary of idiomatic expressions from an American teacher at the school were they worked called "Anglo American School", Mrs. Jacobs, I remember that was her name was the Principal of the Anglo American School, it was not our School I attended a public High School, while the Anglo was private and for the rich student s, anyway to make a long story short, Enrique and I made a plan that I will copy the Dictionary of idiomatic expressions, I copied from the Alphabet letter A to the letter M, and my friend Enrique copied from the letter Q to Z, can you imagine how motivated we were; and the funny thing that happened when we returned the dictionary, we were told to keep it, what a shock after copying so much, it was not for nothing indirectly we benefited learning words; after so much work; anyway by copying we learned more English Idiomatic expressions.

But, before my trip I want you to know the odd things we did to make friends with Americans; I remember we (Enrique and I) had a friend in the American Embassy in La Paz, Bolivia so we asked the secretary for the name of the person, the marine guards did not say a thing; after we went to different floors we found the person and talked a lot and then we stop in every floor until some American civilian police stop us and interrogated us they though we took a bomb or something like that, the good side out a bad thing they interrogated us in English which was nice for us, we looked as practice, but I have to admit they were very mean to us, this lasted like half an hour, they finally realized we were telling the true and let us go.

We also wrote a letter to President Eisenhower that at that time, He was the President of the U.S.A.; asking him to help us to come to the USA, that my friend and I desired to study there; we were that motivated; to our surprise we received a letter from President Eisenhower advising us to apply to certain institutions; we were that crazy. Eventually my friend Enrique had a scholarship to a University in the USA, I was accepted without a Scholarship 3 years late to the Milwaukee School of Engineering,

The trouble was I came from a poor family had no money for the ticket I was glad that mother sold her house in a little town called Uncia for about $600 I was told; the ticket was like $350 and my tuition was $250 dollars a quarter; which did not leave with much anyway after collecting more money; I had some from my other scholarship in La Paz given by "la casa Patiño" a Bolivian millionaire that money selling the mineral Tin during the second World War; he helped students I cashed that; it was not much scholarship that amounted like $200 not much for the USA, but good for La Paz, I was at the time in the University of La Paz called "Universidad de San Andres" I was in my third year of Petroleum Engineering. The Patiño scholarship covered my food at the University at the Cafeteria at the University. At that time, I was living with relatives in La Paz.

To make a long story short, I had my student visa, and left for the USA on September, 1958; after I landed on Miami,I remember I took Greyhound bus from Miami to Milwaukee; when the bus stopped in Mississippi, and had to go to the bathroom in 1958 they were two bath rooms with this name " Whites only " and the other was "Colored only" in my case being from South America did not know which one to get; I was more brown than White or Negro; so I did not care I got the fastest one; that was America then.

Three weeks before school started, I was happy and unhappy at the same time I knew I did not have enough money except for 3 quarters not even for a year, things were so tight at that time I guess rent for room was $7.0 a week; I was fortunate I had a part time work at school we cleaned Boston Store; I had to vacuum and sweep, at the beginning I did not like because never in my life I did vacuum of floors in Bolivia for one thing in my home there was no rugs. So, by working, I had enough money to pay for my room and eat in the restaurant in State Street four blocks from school; later on, I had a job in this restaurant peeling potatoes but the way my roommate a student from Switzerland his name was Fritz Minder helped to peel potatoes for free, because he had money for School, but was a good Friend, I will explain later the ordeal he had when I was in the second semester.

Anyway, I was late in my tuition payment so I was called to the office of Vice-President of MSOE. I will not mention any names; but he really castigated me out loud; I remembered his words he said: "You foreign students come here without any money for tuition"; meaning me of course I am sure the other had money or rich parents, my answer was the reason is that you advertise too much and happened to read the opportunity to come to the States; which I always dreamed. I knew he was going to kick me out and saw myself already going back to Bolivia, but it did not occur.

After I told him I did not eat for 3 days I was surviving just with coffee and sweet rolls he felt sorry for me and took me to the school Cafeteria and gave me frozen steaks and gave me a job cleaning blackboard at MSOE (Milwaukee School of Engineering). That helped me a lot to pay my rent, buy books etc.

Anyway, I forgot to mention that the company in La Paz, Bolivia, which was a mining company that was supposed to help me financially, I was promised by gentleman that said just go for the six months and after they were supposed to help me with tuition money but after being 3 months at school I got a letter stetting the they went into bankruptcy and no help was coming; actually did not make sad because my goal was always to come to the United States of America; so I continued until I was running out of tuition money; one of my classmates felt sorry for me; I remember he said Carlos I made money when I was in the merchant marine in South America I will give you $500 that I do not have to pay or repay if I want; anyway that kept me for another 6 months.

During School I had a friend a student from Switzerland he spoke Spanish also, I mentioned him 2 paragraphs before, we were roommates he was good in electronics he said he worked with before in Venezuela,his name was Fritz Minder, He was my roommate the same guy that helped me to peel potatoes for the restaurant, he used to come to help me to peel potatoes at night for the restaurant, somehow a very strange thing happen, one morning when I went to school like 8:00AM I saw him in his bed, I though he did not had classes, when I came back at 12 he still was sleeping, but I noticed something strange he did not answer to my calling, and when I tried to wake him up did not respond I saw some blood in the bed, I called 911, later I found out he wanted to commit suicide, he cut his wrist, because of romantic problems, that I did not know.

Fritz Minder eventually decided to return to Switzerland, He gave me his car, it was a small car, was standard transmission, and used the car for a while . then when I needed money for the green card I sold it I got like $ 600 that helped a lot.

I almost forgot, during my attending MSOE School, I was robbed one night that I happen to go to the tavern a block away from my Apartment. I think what happened I saw the bartender my 10,000 pesos Bolivianos ; which was equivalent to maybe $5 dollars in 1959, so two Mexican Americans that happen to be there talk to me in Spanish and since I did not have friends at the time, they offered me to introduce some girls, and when I walked with them I was attacked and bitten that to the point I had a black eye, they took my money which it was not more than $10 dollars and run away; I remember when I went back to my room putting ice on my eye I happen to see a Policeman outside the street making a telephone call with phones they were just for the Police, and had a suspect with him; which when I went to complain to the Policeman I saw that was one of the man that robbed me, so the policeman took him to jail because he had a big record; I remember when we took the honey wagon,(police car) ; he kept telling me to forgive him, that he was going to pay me double he said his mother will pay me, he told me in Spanish, but I felt he had to pay for breaking the law, anyway the Policeman saw him running after they attacked me, and then when I went to court he was given two years in Jail in the city of Milwaukee. For what I saw he will be sorry to go to jail for $15 or $20 dollars, but it was his record that determined that and I guessed he did not have a lawyer to defend him, though the court in the US assigned one for free; which is a nice thing to have if one cannot afford a lawyer.

Well, as time went by, my teacher of Technical Drawing who was a German Immigrant felt sorry for me about my economic conditions and offered me his house and I continued to go to another school that was cheaper called MATC I went a semester.

The thing I did find out about the family was they were of a religious group called I guess "Church of Christ" if I remember well, they really studied the Bible at least 2 days a week, I was studying myself some Sundays they had their services in the German Language.

I heard a lot of German Language in Mr. Heit house that I started to learn it, a fact that helped me when I was drafted in the American Army; let me elaborate this part of my life.

Mr Heit (I used to call him Herr Heit; Herr for people that know some German Herr means Mr), anyway, he sponsored me to be a resident of the United States, so they change my visa from Student Visa to that of a resident visa; I was 23 at the time; by becoming, a resident I did not know Uncle Joe will draft me, I was not a US citizen yet at the time, I got the letter that that I was being drafted in the American Army a fact that I did not mind; I always saw myself in my mind being in the Army when I saw American army movies I imagine me being there; so it did actually happen.

I had my basic training at Leonard Wood, Army Basic Training in Missouri, for eight weeks, then the Army sent me to School for Radio Repair in Fort Hood, Kentucky . Due my electrical training at MSOE., that helped. After graduation before I was sent to Germany, the Vietnam war was going at that time, I remember in a hall, the Army officer said anybody that volunteers for Vietnam will get another $100 on top of our salary which was like $ 100 a month, I did not raise my hand I knew better to volunteer for war.

While, I was in Mr. Heit house I met a Girl in a church, in Milwaukee, just in case in different church it was an Anglican; so during my romance with Nancy, I made a mistake of smoking; I was warned in advance that if I smoke and bring the smell to the House, He will kick me out one day and came home with the smell of cigarettes a fact that caused me to leave the house, Mr. Heit did not appreciate, and like a good German He meant what he said and kick me out, it was my fault, I was learning to smoke and never really got the habit, never really learned to smoke to this day, I learned to drink Beer, because in Milwaukee were a lot of beer Brewers, I remember at that time Schlitz was the popular Beer, it costed in 1958 just ten cents a glass. Herr Heit did not like any vices, in his house; it was forbidden to see TV and women did not use lipsticks; in my opinion they over did it.

Anyway, after I moved, the Army drafted me for Basic Training to Fort Leonard Wood in the State of Missouri; it was tough but I survived the 8 long weeks; after that I was send to Fort Knox to go to school for radio repair; which I accomplished

Fort Knox was, were soldiers learned how to use Tanks it was a very nice barracks and had good food at least for me; the rest of the soldiers missed McDonald's which there was no comparison the food in the Army was good, must be the youth they had, like my son that was born in the USA, with my Bolivian wife, after I left the Army, Young people always liked McDonald's which is very American to the point that one find McDonalds all over the world; it becomes the American influence I was surprised they had in Bolivia, country that I was born, when I returned for vacation in 1994.

After finishing Basic Training, I was sent to Fort Knox, Kentucky; where I learned to repair Army Radios, at that time in 1962, radios still used Tubes not transistors that came later. By the way, for the reader information I was drafted in 1962 to 1964; at that time 1962 was era of the Vietnam War. I remember they offered more money like $100 if we volunteer for Vietnam; my orders were to go to Germany; so I did not volunteer; a fact that I am glad; in my opinion that war had no clear mission and was product of the Cold War with the Communists Countries; like Russia and China.

Anyway, I took a Navy Ship to go to Germany from

New York it took eleven days and eleven nights to cross the Atlantic Ocean; I remember the immensity of the Ocean the color changes from dark Blue to sometimes Dark Green. The trip lasted eleven days.

While in the Ship, I took advantage of the long trip to go to Ship library to get a book to learn more German. I had sea sickening, that was the bad part of the trip on the Atlantic Ocean.

I had an idea of the German Language since as, I explained before in the house I lived for 6 months in Milwaukee the family spoke German and pay attention and got a book to learn at that house; so I learned a little bit and more in the ship; a fact that help me a lot. I remember when I was in Erlangen, Germany,City that I was stationed it was a tank outfit to be exact the Fourth Division; I remember when we took a jeep with a Capitan and three enlisted men; we got lost in Furth the next town, we were going to another American barracks, I became handy with my broken German I asked a German Police and got the right directions, I knew German more than anybody else in the Jeep; the Captain got impressed and we got to our destination in the city of Furth; a fact that made my happy at least for that moment that I could be useful.

After being stationed in the city of Erlangen, I was in Headquarters Company and my job was to repair Army radios, I was trained for that job in Fort Knox. Eventually I had my first pass to go to town in Erlangen which was a beautiful small city so I visited the GI bars, we went in civilian clothes,they were taverns where the G.I went, I had a bad experience that night as I was leaving I saw a couple of drunk GI one that looked Latin was kicking the Taxi which was a Mercedes Benz ; I noticed most of the Taxies were Mercedes Benz, and they were Black in color; I saw the driver came out with a steel bar the people left, somehow when I was going back to the barracks the same Taxi driver stopped me, and 2 guys tried to force me in the Taxi because they thought I was the Latin guy that kicked the door of the Merced's Taxi; so I fought them and run away one followed me I heard a noisy like a small gun shot, I guess the shot missed me .then I got to my bus and when I went to the barracks they were waiting me do I told the guard these two guys were trying to beat me ; and I did not even know them, as I said it was my first time in Town; so we went to the main-office and there the German Police, had an office in the American Barracks, they concluded, it was a mistaken identity, so we all went to the German Police and American Military after they heard my story the Judge said if I was going to put charges, I said no; so the guy that I guess shot me, talked to me in German which by that time I understand the familiar conversation, he said he was sorry " Ich tut mir lied" (meaning I am sorry) that he was given me his wrist watch, I did not take it, so I said it is ok; he became so happy that he kissed my hand; I knew it was all a mistaking identity.

So much for the first pass to Town in Erlangen, it did not discourage I keep going and visiting more German places so I could learn more German. The city of Erlangen was half hour from the city of Nuremberg.

After a while, I went to school to learn German the

Army asked for volunteer soldiers to learn some German, so Americans could get along better with native Germans; I was sent for two weeks to the city of Neu Ulm close to the city of Munich. I remember vividly the instructors were German that were in the American Army; probably like me that they were drafted also we had a female German teacher; the idea was to teach us as much German in two weeks, they use the method teach German using Pictures and explained in German it was forbidding if possible to use English, during the classes; in my opinion it was a good way to learn a Language.

After graduation, the Army sponsored a dinner, where German Girls were invited, the woman were secretaries or probably volunteers, the idea was that of the say 20 Army men, will pick a Lady, take her coat and use German to talk to them, I was very good for that, because I used my not so good German.. So during dinner, we used more German, plus the women did not know English also, so it was good for me so I could practice and also my Army classmates,

The German course was only two weeks, 8 hours a day, we had books and home work every night, I remember during the dinner with Ladies, a Captain asked me Hey Carlos how do say this or that in German, because I was more fluent than the rest.

So, in weekends, I went to German Restaurants so I could use my vocabulary in German I made a friend with a German soldier who did not know too much English that help me

Well the whole idea was that I learn German and maybe I will have a German Girl Friend, unfortunately I met a Girl from Spain who was a nice Lady she was working in the city of Furth; her name was Laura, at that time they were a lot of foreign workers from Spain in Germany that worked and returned to their countries with some money When they made enough money to return to Spain. At that time Franco was the President of Spain..

At that time, Spain was in a bad economic situation, that is why Spaniards worked in German factories, that is when I met the Spanish lady called Laura, she always said she was a Catalan, trying to differentiate from the average Spanish. As now Cataluña is trying to get its independence from Spain., I noticed they use word more connected to French and English. As an example the call forquilla, for fork.

I remember, I went to Barcelona on of the reasons was to meet the mother of Laura that lived in Barcelona. I did find the town, it reminded of Bolivian towns, one thing I noticed that people did not knock the door at night, they clapped their hands, and the noisy was enough, for somebody to open say at midnight, when it was dark.

I stayed 2 weeks in Spain, to get to Barcelona my train pass through Switzerland, I noticed that people talk 3 languages, Italian. German and Spanish, in reality that is fact of Life in Switzerland.

My real test, in German came when I met a German freulein (girl) in the train and talked in German and she liked me she become my date for that day after some beers in Furth I took her to the American barracks in Erlangen,where we had a night club where there was music and beer and spirits; the band sang American tunes even if they did not know English they learned the music and sang using phonetics and did a good job so we, I did ask the band, anyway we danced and so on it was a Saturday night; as she was leaving when we were kissing I heard a noisy made by some Negro soldiers so I told the Girl to go now I was afraid the group of soldiers will take advantage of her because it was dark and outside so my friend left and never saw her again; although she wrote me a letter and that was the end of my experience. By the way I got a picture from her.

I remember, when I was stationed in Germany, those were the years of the cold war, we had maneuvers every month my company went to Grafenwhor (not sure I am spelling right) but I am sure 90 % the name was close to the name I use.; Grafenwhor was close to Czech Republic ;to be exact I was the 4th Division; was part of the 7th Army; we always went to the border close to Czech Republic at that time we assumed that Russians will come this way in a future war. Anyway that was the drill every month for 15 months while I was in Erlangen.

Almost forgot, after maneuvers with the German Army and English Army, we got at night together for a beer, I remember me being from Bolivia and drafted in the US Army I was the middle of a table on my left were English soldiers and in my right was a German soldier, The one on the right told in my ears that do not like the Germans and the other on was vice versa, so I decided to talk to both of them and wound up after more beers, I made them shake hands like friends belonging to NATO, together against the Soviets, as the Soviets were taking nation after nation under the Communism influence, like Latvia, Hungary, Lithuania etc.

Also, my job consisted of repairing radios that was brought to the shop; this was the time radio used vacuum tubes, it was exciting; as I was leaving by March 1964 transistorized radios were coming to Headquarters Company; that was my company at that time.

I was discharged in New York I got my papers and some money, not much enough to stay one night in New York and then go to Milwaukee; I remember in New York when I went dancing you had to pay the girl like $5 dollars to keep you company while you bought drinks for her and you it was plain robbery in my opinion, but it was better than be alone. Eventually, I returned to Milwaukee and started looking for a job around 1964, finally I found a good job at Evinrude Motors it was the best paid job, because it had a Union in the factory so they paid decent wages.

I went from a Platter helper to became an Electrical technician, I really liked my company I did my best I worked for 30 years, until I had a knee replacement I remembered how my legs used to get tired going from one shop to another, eventually after the knee replacement the company supplied me with a cart run by battery it was we called a Cushman, finally I retired with 30 years and out. I was 57 years old then.

I really liked the Company I worked, I did my best to help, we manufactured outboard motors, used in boats all over the world.

I noticed, that most of the piece workers worried more for the quantity of the pieces than the quality, that was the time the Japanese had fewer errors in his cars and less mistakes; America manufacturing turned to more serious performance, and made great cars and outboard motors.

The part, I forgot to mention is I married my second wife, She is from Ouro, Bolivia when I went for vacation to my Mother in Oruro, Bolivia she was 90 years old already, I will tell my story because it is unusual, when I was walking with my nephew in Oruro, I saw two girls walking I the street called 6 de October, (six of October), I remember I said to Angel (my nephew) the following : If I marry again (I was divorced at that time) would marry a woman like Her, 20 minutes later, I saw them buying Ice cream and we met them there, the woman I marry later in 3 weeks her name was Yalila, it worked pretty good and had no trouble with the American Embassy, because I was already a veteran from the US Army. The marriage was successful she was 20 years younger than me, we are married now for 36 years as of today January, 24, 2016...

My first wife was from Milwaukee, her name is Nancy I had a Daughter with her called Annelise, I was proud of my Daughter because she graduated as in Bioengineering in Berkeley, California with a PHD.

Now she works at Stanford University, she is married

with one boy and a Daughter, his name is Max and the girls is Katya. In another relationship she a boy named Finn., he is 3years old now as 2016

My Bolivian wife, became a Registered Nurse in Milwaukee, after she learned English, and works at the Veterans Hospital. And she will retire in 2 years from now today is February 2016.

In Evinrude Motors, my job was as an Electrical Technician I took care of the Machine Shop, latter my department was the Foundry in the foundry; at that time we made our crankshafts from scratch, starting in the molds and then using steel at higher temperatures and the workers in the foundry damped the hot steel to shape the crankshafts, heat treated and then machined it was a complete elaborate task; and my job was to keep the machines running at least electrically, because maintenance took care of the plumbing and machine repair and Millwrights that took care of the conveyors etc.

I worked with 2 electricians from Latvia, and one German at Evinrude Motors, the one that show me the ropes, his name is, Janis Bergmanis, I hope he is alive, he must be in his 90 by now; I tried to look for him and no luck. The other Foundry Electrician was also from Latvia his name was Janis Mintikis, he is deceased now.; also I worked with a German Electrician. his name was Willy Jerke that immigrated after the second world war. He used to tell He was in the German Army, very nice and efficient Electrical Technician.

I remember how close I was to get killed when I was fixing a robot called "Unimate" it was a machine that rotated at high speeds 360 degrees and has arms to pick up parts and put in certain places and pick up after the parts got the refractory materials, anyway to make a long story short, somehow I believed the careless operator, pressed a button when I was repairing it hit my ears half an inch more it would have hit me in the head and probably brake the skull, I complained about that operator that I still have doubts if he did purposely, I was bleeding from my ears when I complained the safety coordinator.

I cheated death that time. I am talking in the years around 1990.

In 1994 I had a knee replacement on the left leg, I was close to retirement anyway I had 29 years by then, and one needed 30 years and out, I was fortunate that the company supplied me with a Cushman (golf cart) to move around the shop. That helped a lot because I could not walk with an artificial knee at that time and my trade it was hard to perform specially to knee to connect motors, which were located mostly on the floor.

Before I forget, I want to mention, a situation at work, since I was in maintenance we had a Maintenance Supervisor, who was not much of Supervisor, He was sitting on his desk, I remember we had fire on air conditioner unit on the roof, I mentioned the fire he did not get up from his desk and asked me to get the millwrights, which that was not my Job, it was his as a supervisor. This just one of the many things I observed.

A few months later there was a retirement Party for the Foundry Supervisor, his name is or was Mr. Pitt, I worked in the Foundry and was my friend, most of the invited were Supervisors I was the only union worker for what I noticed,under the influence of the beer, when I saw the Planta Manager, his name is Harry Wilson,I asked him this question : Do you know what your Supervisors performance, plus I told him that I work for the principle not the money, though both go together, I complained about the lack of Interest of the Maintenance Supervisor, after he heard my complain, he said he would look into, maybe ask the other Supervisor what their opinion of the Maintenance Supervisor..

Anyway, the following day, I felt bad for talking against my boss, but in America we are free to supposedly to give our assessment.; anyway, the following day all the supervisors were proud of me, because they did not have the guts to complain, and they were given me a quarter to buy myself a coffee for telling the complaint to the plant Supervisor.

After three weeks, I happen to cross The plant manager, He was young and always wells dressed, with a white shirt and a tie; he stopped and He said the following: Carlos I am not forgetting what you told me About the Maintenance Supervisor, and then a week later, the maintenance Supervisor was demoted to third shift; I felt bad but, I said it now I know the beer gave more guts, which is the way alcohol works on human beings. Unfortunately 2 years later the Maintenance Supervisor, his name was Gene Bahr, he passed away.

As a hobby I became an Amateur Radio operator, more normally know as a Ham Radio operator, for which one need a license, I had to study courses in electronics I got to the last license of Extra my call sign is KG9FC. I made contacts with Spain and Cuba, that made me happy.

But with computer revolution, my interest in Ham Radio diminished a lot; but I still have my radios in my Basement, I was active in a 2-meter band., which is popular in amateur clubs in Milwaukee.

I got social security pension when I reached 62 with disability because of the artificial knee; and got a small pension for 30 years; which could not be enough to survive social security helped a lot. As I am writing this diary in a way about my experiences in Milwaukee, Wisconsin I am 65 years old in this year of 2002.

The year 2001 was a bad year for America, because of the attack in New York by terrorists most of them from Saudi Arabia; which shows to me maybe they resent the American bases over there not sure but they seem to send a message and Bin Laden is also a Saudi, may by this time our forces will find him nothing yet today March, 9th 2002.

Tough later President Obama and his cabinet did find that Osama Bin Laden was living I Pakistan, and the US sent 2 helicopters at night, and killed Osama Bin Laden, probably the Pakistan Army knew about it but, the pretended they did not know, the Us Government did not let them also, because according to the CIA they could not be trusted.

Anyway, President Obama accomplished that, I was very proud of President Obama and still I am, because I was a volunteer when he run for the Presidency in 2008 of the most powerful country in the world.

As good news, my daughter Annelise will have a baby boy around July ten, according what the Doctor said to my daughter; consequently I am very excited to being a Grand Pa

What amazed me is that I guessed right the sex of the baby before the Doctor determined with a scan.

I remember one day after the wedding my daughter, and husband were invited to a downtown bar in Seattle; my daughter was sitting next to me in the bar so she noticed after two beers my voice changes, she gave me a lecture to the fact that I have the genes the Indian people, I might have some Indian since I come from Bolivia place of the Incas civilization in other words we get drunk fast; she was right I knew all the time, but his time she pinpointed, and that when I said as of today no more alcohol because I used to go to the bar at least three time a week and always get out drunk. So I said to Annelise ok I will not drink anymore until the boy is born and you are going to have a son, a fact that I was right, his name is going to be Maxwell, I am writing now is May 25th I remember it was memorial week end in the 2002; She is 7 and half months pregnant now. My daughter is an assistant professor in Chemical Engineering at Northwestern University in Evanston, Ill.

Now is June 27, 2002 had not a call from Anita; (I used to call her in a Spanish name for Annelise); I am sure she does not want me to worry; but I expect next week according to the Doctor she told me it will be by July 8, I have a feeling it will be by July 10.

Well, my daughter had the baby boy on July 2, 2002 his name is Maxwell, but we call him just Max his actual name given to him by his parents is Maxwell Sanger Oleg Jardetzky.

His grandparents from the husband side Ted has roots in Russia as you can see with Oleg Jardetzky.

Max now is more 2 months and is beautiful boy, I heard yesterday he had his first laugh when Anita called me.. I called my Daughter Anita ;that was September 15. I was sick for more than 16 days with abdominal pain I lost 5 pounds my Doctor cannot pinpoint the problem I had x rays, Cat Scans and finally colonoscopy I guess that help the most, everything was normal. The problem of my stomach started when I ate shrimp and a friend called on Sunday to the bar I did not feel like drinking beer on Sunday after I got drunk on Saturday, anyway when I got home I felt sick and the following day I was with cramps, I had what is called irritable Bowel Syndrome slowly and normally. I think my problem is with the liver two brothers of mine died in Bolivia with stomach problems they developed Pancreatitis, I so I think the curse is following me. So I decide never to drink beer again; I did quit for 7 months I dedicated to max when my daughter was pregnant for two months, but after Max was born and my birthday came on July 16, I celebrated with beer and that was the beginning till I got sick.

Plus, I have a friend I met in my friends Bar called "Douglas Inn, in Milwaukee my friend was an alcoholic, his name is John, the bar was almost across my work Evinrude Motors, the name of the bar is, still Douglass Inn; he finally is working he did some work in my house he put linoleum on my kitchen floor, because he felt compelled to do it for me for free because I had helped him in the days he needed help, and was grateful to me.

My friend John will only work if he drinks beer I guess I one day he drank 24 cans he will not eat until very late, it is the only person I never seem him drunk and perform that well he painted my kitchen with no problem, I had to drink some to keep him company maybe all those days were the beginning of my problem with the abdominal pain.

My friend, was homeless he used to sleep on his truck he had an old Chevrolet, even the night he worked in the kitchen I offered him a bed, nevertheless he went to his truck and slept this it was in July I and was a hot night, still I cannot understand why, when I asked him why will not use a bed his answer was "Who Can I be if not myself", I remember that expression very well.

The reader might ask himself why I mention a homeless alcoholic man, because an America not everybody lives well, they are people that cannot make or the vice got the best of them. Since this book is a memoir, that is what impressed me, and show the reader what life is, and I observed as part of my Life in Milwaukee.

My friend John did a good job, painted the kitchen and

good ; I was afraid of that because in Bolivia people that live not all but the majority and it happened to me too inevitably they get sick of the stomach, just like Americans get the revenge of Montezuma when they visit Mexico.

Anyway, he stayed for 8 months in Milwaukee before we helped him to go to Berkeley, California, a relative helped him to get a jog but he only worked 30 hours so we started help him again specially when he got to move again, he was not happy with Dave an old ex land lord he was a guy that watched TV smoking pot I remember the peculiar smell of Pot when I used to visit my son in Berkeley.

By this time, my daughter of my previous marriage was divorcing her husband of 6 years, a fact that made me very unhappy even as write tonight it is 2:43 am my wife will come from the hospital work by 4 am, she is hard working lady and helps a lot to pay the bills plus the mortgage; she is planning to retire in 7 years from now, the date June 28, 2008.

So life continues, although sometimes I feel lonely when my wife is working long hours ; but I keep myself busy with my computers I just installed some software to learn Russian words, I got interest on that after Sergey he is from Ulan Ude, Russia, area clos to Mongolia, he lived for 2 months with me I figured if a German Immigrant helped me with the green card, I will help Sergey from Russia, the reason I helped him because the people he knew in Milwaukee when He came as exchange worker from Russia to learn how to repair Television Sets. And when He returned as a tourist later on none of his American friends volunteered to give him a hand, so I decided to help, I thought since after the cold war America and Russia should corporate after avoiding a nuclear war in 1962, during the Cuban crisis.

I helped him to get a driver license, he could not work in America even if he was an electrical Engineer he came as a tourist and could not stay in America unless he gets a resident visa; last time I talked to him he went to Florida in the car I sold him very cheap to help him, he obtained an asylum visa

One thing I noticed in the Russian Mechanics' that live and work in Milwaukee, close to my house I used to take my son's car for repair, and when I took Sergey, I noticed they discriminated Sergey because he was not a White Russian, was with Mongolic features, that is when I realized America is less discriminatory compared to some European countries.

I learned some Russian sentences when I took him to the bar I has a note book to write down with useful sentences. Plus, I learned some Cyrillic alphabet.

As part of my life, my pet parakeet his name was Marvin, I had him for 3 years I got so used to him that it was a shock one Friday when I came back, I usually start talking to him before I open the door and he used to answer with his familiar noise, but he was not on his cage usually he stays on top, I had my cellular phone in my hand Was trying to call that Marvin flew but I found him drowned in the water in the toilet, I was so desperate that I pick him up while I was holding my cellular phone ; all I remember my phone was wet and Marvin was death ; I put him outside on the sun to no avail, I knew he was dead plus the water had Clorox in the water, I was so desperate that I wanted to get drunk I took a beer from the refrigerator, I proceeded to bury him on my garden I was crying a lot ; after that I took his picture and went to the tavern that is close to my house I mentioned the people that I was sad because of Marvin and proceeded to get drunk to kill the pain; I really loved the bird ; I remember how he looked at me I knew he sensed me even when he bit me it was with love.

Three days later my tubing under my Isuzu broke and lost my brakes I was lucky it happened before I took the freeway; that could have serious consequences like being a fatality; I really believe that my parakeet died for me; I reburied my bird because some animals in my garden opened the grave and guess they ate part of Marvin, my brother in law made a deeper hole and put Marvin in a plastic container and he buried again this time for good, I hope.

Changing the theme, I feel very happy that Barack Obama won the election in 2008 and is the 44th President of the USA. He will be inaugurated on January 20th; today is November 25th. ; and I felt so happy.

Today August 2010, I have started to drink beer again after I quit for a year.

Also after this date I stopped writing my memoirs. So today November 16 I start writing again.

Well, I want to write about another Friend his name

is Frank, He is the same age as me and also a veteran of the US Army; I met him like 15 years ago in the bar called "Hideaway" first I remember his wife used to smoke and also drink eventually she died like 10 years ago, but her husband continue drinking almost every day I used to see his Truck it was a blue Ford, I could not believe every day ;sometimes I went to drink with him I tried to mention to slow down but his answer always was: what I am going to do in the house . In my case I have a hobby I am a ham radio amateur; plus I like to read; go to movies etc. No way I will drink like my friend Frank.\

Eventually, Frank got sick he was in the hospital and then in rehab nursing home for a while; I went to visit him. Then eventually he left the rehab and I start seeing his truck again every day; I knew eventually he will get sick; the last time I drink with him and his son and daughter in law on a Saturday; I found out he wound up in the hospital after a month I found out he had an operation in the intestines it is called colostomy where he has a bag in the stomach; that made me very unhappy; during this time my Son Carl that lives in Berkeley decided to take Mathematics to be exact the course was Calculus and he ask me some problems ; because I did study many years ago Calculus as an Engineer course in Bolivia, South America and it came easy to me I bought a used book from Amazon I installed Fax and I used to fax the problems so he could learn . I knew my son will flank because to study Calculus you need discipline, and no drinking or use pot; I am talking about my son, I never learned how to smoke, At that time I quit drinking to have a clear mind plus the problem of my friend Frank I decide to quit forever, because Frank is the same age as mine 75 years old; he appears older than me.

Today February 12, I visited Frank I noticed he lost like 40 pounds, he was in a good health, but he was good enough to let me visit him, He lives with Daughter that works as a teacher, and Fran is most of the time alone, He is an Army veteran also like me and the same age, He is 80 and still drives his old Ford. I was glad to talk to him.

So today, I am writing this after 4 months of no beer and any alcohol and still doing the exercises that are a lot; I knew my son will not make he had a D the first test and the second he flunked so he decided to drop it; it was the best ; it was a crazy idea from Carl to take Calculus because he does not have discipline to study I used to stay till 2 AM every night doing the exercises, it was too much that sent by priority mail, finally he drop last week and myself have more time to read the New York Times; I enjoy this paper.

This Month December 2015, I found my Friend Enrique, the friend from High School in Oruro, Bolivia . Enrique and I learned English as I mentioned at the beginning of my memoir, he found me in linked, and we chatted using skype, after 60 years; it was fun to remember our youth in Oruro, Bolivia.

When I told him, I started a book 10 years ago, he advised me to write every day, and that is why I am starting today on January 7, 2016, we chatted by using skype,I saw him and he saw me, I noticed he has more white hair than me, he is 79 now I am 80years old. We remember the crazy things we did to learn the English Language in Oruro, Bolivia.

In Milwaukee, with lots of snow, this is the day that President Obama talked about guns in America, and by executive order he, implemented that people the buy and sell should use the check every buyer for criminal or mental pass, that way it will not be easier to buy guns, specially is in the Gun shows, I went once many years ago and I realized already how easy will be for bad gut to buy gun, with little background check up; as a matter of fact I did buy a small 38 revolver, and when I was teaching my wife how o shoot it did not work, I was working at Evinrude Motors,at the time, so some friend of mine checked the gun and found out that was defective. So my friend bought, very cheap and try to fix himself for he knew about guns.

This is what I remember today, so I will continue to write as my friend Henry advised me to do.

Today, is January 16, 2016, Milwaukee still cold, and people are happy because the Green Bay Packers are in the playoffs, next game in Arizona tomorrow Saturday 17.

Unfortunately the Green Bay Packers lost and got eliminated. No playoff no more. At least in 2016..

Last two days I had an appointment with my Oculist,6-month checkup. specially for Glaucoma. Because there some history in my Family my sister Hilda in Bolivia had Glaucoma, though she lived to the age of 94, just like my Mother. I do not have Glaucoma but the cataract got worse on my left eye, my Doctor wants to operate, but I asked for another prescription for long distance on my left eye, by the way I am 80 years as at this moment January, 22, 2016, plus I want to finish my memoir first, just in case something happen to my eye, though cataract operations are mostly safe, I will wait until I finish this year my memoir of how I came to the USA and my experience and things I observed.

I am one of the believers of the saying "If it works do not fix it "so far my eyes are working so-so, but I do not drive at night, I do not trust myself to read signs on the street..

So, today I told my friend Enrique, He is in La Paz, Bolivia I told him, that I have to finish my memoir this year, because I am running out of time, I am already 80 and waiting for an Eye operation, whose outcome nobody knows except for the probability that will be Ok.

I was a volunteer in 2008, for Barack Obama for President; I was very happy, I liked him because he was a very intellectual President, only in America Barack being an Afro American can become President in a nation that still has discrimination, but America still has less discriminations than any country in the world; that what make America great.

I met Barack Obama wife Mitchel when she came to Milwaukee, to help Obama. I remember I introduced myself like this; I am Carlos from Bolivia and a supporter of your Husband, and please tell Barack to concentrate on the Latinos in Texas, this was during the election and did,

Barack before he was President got the Latino vote in his favor.

He took the troops from Iraq which was good, that was one of the reason He had elected, though lately, we have another problem with Isis, anyway we did leave the majority of troops. In my opinion President Obama came at the right time; he looks in the future to talk to Iran, a very important country that is essential for peace in that area; If Romney would have won, he promised Israel that will help Israel, I remember I read in the New York Times Magazine the plans of Israel to attack Iran, a war that would put America in a senseless war that we cannot afford.

In fact, that is one of the reasons oil is cheap, so cheap that affected badly Venezuela, Russia etc.

Today January 27, 2016. I would be in the USA for 56 years, since I arrived to the USA with a student visa. Now, I am a veteran of this Country and very proud of it.. I joined the American Legion in Menomonee Falls. Wi ; very close to my house in Milwaukee. Post 382.

I never thought that to write a memoir was going to be easy, especially when you get older in my case 80 years, sometimes I forgot the past experiences I had, but the only reason I am writing this book, is to let the American reader know how some immigrants had difficulties in coming to America, and become a person of good and to be a good citizen of this country.

In my case, I always wanted to come to America, maybe

because I learned the Language, I remember my brother in Bolivia that worked in the University in my home town Oruro, Bolivia that book was a history book, I remember I memorized the Gettysburg Address of Abraham Lincoln, to the point that I memorized it all this before I came to America, also read the constitution of the USA and memorized the preamble, all this was in that history book, my brother Jorge gave to me.

Sometimes, I surprised myself the things we did with Enrique, in Oruro we study the Jehovah Witness Bible in English, the reason was more to learn more the English Language.

And when I was in another city in La Paz Bolivia in the University of San Andres, studying Petroleum Engineering, in Laz Paz there was an American church a Methodist Church, were the American Embassy personnel attended, I used to attend every Sunday just to understand the sermons, I remember I was the only Bolivian there, they were very friendly as American church goers always are.

The reason I mention this events of my life, I feel it a story that should be shared, with American reader, the things people do to come to America. My reason was I always liked to come to America.

I remember when President Nixon came to La Paz Bolivia, around 1956 I was in the University, I approached his car and shook hand with me, I remember I said Mr. Nixon welcome to Bolivia, and he said oh you speak English and I remember he said why don't you come to the USA, and I said to him : "It is my golden dream", and it really happened, like I am mentioning in this book now.

Since I do not have enough pages for a book, I decided maybe I should forget writing my memoir, because my coming to America and the time in the Army only cover like 16 pages.

Anyway I decide maybe I should keep writing what is happening in this election time in the 2016, with Trump really wining, In my opinion I believe He will be the next President of this great country, like Trump says all the time "we will make America great again", and he means it.

The only thing I do not like about Trump if he gets to be President, He wants to kick 11 million illegals, that would not be practical, I was thinking who is going to cook breakfast for Trump in the Greek Restaurants, like in Milwaukee city where I the cooks are Mexicans, not a practical. Trump idea.

Today February 29, 2016 Trump is fighting with Marco Rubio with insults from each side, Rubio promises to repeal everything that President Obama Care, I like Obama care, which in my opinion is not a good idea, it is too late now because they are millions already enrolled;

Since I do not have enough material of my experiences of how I had to endure to learn English in Bolivia and my life in America, I will write about America especially in the elections of 2016. Just a few minutes ago I saw Romney a leader of the Republic Party call Trump a Phony and not good for America as President, in my opinion Romney is right .Trump is to extreme and violent that might create more problems for America, he is Macho type, the other candidate Ted Cruz is a guy that will not compromise, if he has to shut the government of the USA for what he believes he will do as he brags himself, that is not good, a President he has to compromise, otherwise he is one way street, I am talking about Ted Cruz.

Of the 3 candidates Rubio will be the best, at least he believes in immigration, and not kicking 11 million peoples like Trump, that will cause a financial problem to America.

What I really want to write is election the Democrats will not win the White House. it is time for the Republicans the reason I said is that I my more than 50 years in the USA, I have learned how the mood of the American voters change, After of Obama I am sure they want a Republic President. So far Trump is ahead of Rubio and Cruz.

Today, March13.2016 . this election is getting ugly,two days ago protesters tried to interrupt the Trump really, actually it was so violet that Trump cancelled if, I guess it is Trump fault also, for he encouraged his supporters to punch them on the face, those are the words he used.

Unfortunately, the way I see Trump will win, it all depend if he wins Florida and Ohio in two days, then He will be unstoppable.

As of today April 23, trump won Florida, lost in my State Wisconsin, won New York, his chances are getting better, even if Cruz won Colorado, so far they are separated by around 300 votes between Trump and Cruz .Tomorrow April 26 They will vote in Pennsylvania, Virginia and another 3 states, I will mentioned later as the days go by.

One event that sounds very undemocratic, I heard that Cruz and Kasich join force to block Trump or take votes from him, so he will not get closer to 1,300, Trump accuses that elections in America are rigged, in a way he is right., like Colorado gave all his voted to Cruz and nobody else.

Today April 26, 2016, Trump won Pennsylvania., actually five States. Hillary Clinton, wins two States, it seems that Hillary will be the Candidate for the Democratic Party., the problem is for the Republicans, some on the Republic Party do not want her as a candidate, but I believe he will be the candidate, because of he being ahead of the other two candidates, and if the people that Republic and did not vote before if they decide to vote will pass the Latinos and Afro America blocks and Trump will win.

Trump has a good foreign Policy, way different than the other Presidents, the way he talks he will be our next President. By the way today, May 3 rd. Trump won Indiana, that make him that he will be the Republic nominee, since Cruz drop out of to be contend ender to Trump.

At this moment, Trump is thanking Indiana and everybody for his triumph, he also acknowledged that Cruz was a hard contender., today also the National Inquirer published that Cruz Father was next to Oswald the person that killed Jack Kennedy, that did not help Cruz..

Anyway, that is over now, Trump will be the candidate to President for the Republic Party. I will keep writing about this election, I enjoy using Microsoft word, that help a lot when one writes a book.

This 2016 elections are the more ugly I have seen, to the point of insults and called each other as lairs, specially between the Republicans Trump against Cruz, Cruz finally gave up and stop campaigning after losing Indiana, which put Trump ahead, and it seems he will be the candidate for the Republic Part, he is so sure I mean Trump that even gave his foreign world Policy, a little drastic to the allies. In a way Trump is right the NATO countries has to pay more of their share, since America is defending them, mostly against the Soviet Union, which is the only country, that can send atomic rockets to America.

This is the worst insulting election I have seen in America, Trump went to the point of insulting the husband of Hillary Clinton, that has nothing to do, anyway he brought Bill Clinton as an abuser of women in the white House, especially with Monica Lewinsky. I

This I consider very law blow to bring the past, to hurt Hillary and that way people will not vote for her; this is in my opinion it seems Trump is so deep in the desire to be President of the USA so badly that, will insult or bring dirty pass to get to be President. And I believe he is smart and manipulator.

As of today. The Speaker of the House Pau Ryan is not endorsing Trump yet, even if they had a meeting yesterday, Ryan said is was a positive meeting.

In my opinion if Trump will win they need to get

together to unify the Republic Party, and if they intend to defeat Hillary Clinton.

For what I observed, they are a lot of institutions and people in the Republic Party and of course the Democratic Party, Hillary is more important than Trump., I noticed last Sunday May 15th The New York Times published a story how Trump treated various women, in my opinion that is personal and not necessary to publish, It is obvious that this paper does not want Trump to become the candidate for President of the United States, but I see the probabilities are in favor of Trump, so it will not be a surprise to me, besides he is closer to get the 1,300 votes he needs, he is 1,100 now, there more states that will vote before July. California is in June.

Today May 20, 2016 Mr. Trump had the endorsement of the RNA (Rifle National Association) a powerful lobby in America, that is a good sign that he might win the elections, his only problem will be the Spanish vote, tough I notices the Spanish vote is not monolithic, I hears some Latins will vote for him, mostly because Trump is supposed to create Jobs; in my opinion Trump has good ideas it is true that America has negative balances with China and Japan, eventually that has to be even or improve.

Good news for trump today May 26th,2016 he got the necessary votes to be the candidate for President for the Republic Party, he must be happy, but he was but was still insulting Hillary Clinton and the Spanish Republic Governor of New Mexico, because she did not attend the ceremonies in her State New Mexico, she is not happy the way Trump plans for the Mexicans that are illegal, 11 million including other nationalities.

They have been anti Trump protests, in California, one week before the primaries. In my opinion the only way that Trump will lose if Republicans that do not like Trump vote for Hillary Clinton.

Trump will definitively be the official candidate for the Republic Party, the problem he will have is with Spanish and African American vote, though Trump keeps saying he will get the Spanish vote, I doubt after he insulted the Mexicans as rapists, actually they help the American economy, the way I see if he kicks the 11 million illegals, who is going to do Trump breakfast in the Greek Restaurants, where the cooks are all Mexican, I know as a fact because I talk to them in Spanish., here in Milwaukee.

At this very moment June 2nd. Hillary is on CNN and said We cannot trust Trump with the nuclear codes, I noticed myself he is belligerent even with press, of course Hillary Clinton has experience in Government she was the Secretary of State, under President Obama. She said a very good opinion if Trump would be elected it will b a historical mistake ; I myself agree.

Trump showed he uses race to denigrate the Judge the is in his case of Trump University, he call the Judge he is bias against Trump because he is Mexican,and Trump is going to build a wall. Actually the Judge was born in Indiana of Mexicans parents, so he is as American as Trump; Trump is a making a mistake of using race, being the candidate to be the American President, I saw and heard Republics disgusted, even Ryan the speaker of the House, those things will handicap Trump, his behavior is not Presidential at all.

Trump reminds of certain men I saw in the Bars when I was drinking, very negative and always picking at the time I was drinking I was an Obama volunteer, 98 % were against Obama; I guess mostly race, because most of them were not educated to understand the background of Obama he was and is very Intellectual, a Lawyer that graduated from the prestigious Harvard. University.

This last comment of Trump, disappointed me if he does nor respects Judge, I am afraid he will be above the law, President Nixon had to accept the Judiciary when he was impeached, but he resigned before that.

Today June 7th. Hillary Clinton had the necessary votes to be the Democratic Candidate for President of the USA like I said before if Americans do not want Trump to win, the alternative and better is Hillary Clinton, personally I will vote for her. The other democrat Bernie Sanders will in a few minutes give speech. Probably accepting the defeat and I hope to help Hillary. So far Sanders did not endorse Hillary yet, even after President Obama endorsed her today June 9th. He said she is the most prepared to be the President of the USA, meaning compared to Trump...

I heard on the Car radio that Sanders will do the best to stop Trump to be President of this great country USA, time will tell, in my opinion if Trump would apologize to the Judge of Mexican descent, he was born in Indiana, that was a mistake for trump to refer that the Judge has bias in the problems of the Trump University, is wrong, he is a federal judge and we know that no one is above the Law in the United States, perhaps the only country that follows what they preach.

Today, June 20, 2016 there was a shooting in Orlando, Florida by a Moslem person that was born in the USA from whose parents were from Afghanistan, he was 29 years old, he killed 50 persons in a Guy bar this is the worst massacre after 9/11.

Very sad situation indeed, president said it was a terror attack, the perpetrator name was Omar, he called 911 to them that he was loyal to ISIS, that explains his criminal behavior; plus he has said according to with nesses that he disliked homosexuals.

Summer, is great in Milwaukee, it is Sunday June 19, just heard on TV, that the GOP or some in the GOP planning to block Trump in the convention, I doubt very much they can do anything, but the news of the son of an Afghan immigrant murdered 49 people, and Trump wants to ban immigrants coming from Syria I am sure that ISIS fill infiltrate people, I guess that helps Tramp and American people will vote for Trump; I myself agree in part that ISIS will infiltrate,they already did in Brussels few months ago with immigrant that went and still going now.

This election 2016 is the first I have seen in the more

than 50 years I am in the Country, when the candidates insult to each other, like Trump reaping this that Hillary is the most crooked candidate, and Hillary making fun of Trump, today she said that Trump will get the nation in recession, that y is very negative I am sure she said so the American people do not vote for Trump, but for her and the Democratic Party.

After the killing of 49 people by Moslem American, the Democrats senator are trying to asks the senate to vote for a Bill no gun if one has a bad criminal record, but unfortunately the Republic Senators that are inclined to RNA are not willing to vote, it has been 13 hours of Filibuster by the Democratic Representatives', my hope that tomorrow something happens, I hope Trump gets involves asking he RNA to be more flexible, Nobody is trying to stop the Second Amendment; for yeas the RNA is not flexible, which is shame, Omar was investigated by the FBI twice and they let it go, and bought an R15, weapon that was used to kill 49 young people, and the Senators still is creating problems. In my opinion the FBI has some responsibility for the Tragedy, maybe they should pass the terrorist list to the Gun Dealers, especially when Omar wanted to buy a body Armor, and the gun dealer told the authorities and nobody follow it.

The FBI says they had no grounds to arrest him, maybe so because he was born in America, but he should have been in a black list, especially when he Omar that wanted to hurt people to his coworkers, and was fired from work with no further consequences.

Today June 28, 2016 Trump gave a Speech in Economics and the things he will do. What surprised me he sounds different and more Presidential, He wants to be President so bad that America will be greater, in my opinion American was always Great.

I was delighted the he sounded more polite and his message was good for his audience.

We will see what happens in November, his probabilities are good so far. Trump is using the book Clinton Cash, were the author points out the Clinton get a lot of money for speeches from India, because Hillary helped in the open relation to the Atomic situation in India, and as a result Indian Millionaires will denote millions to the Clinton Foundation.

Trump used that in his speech, not mentioning India just the cash it went to the foundation.

On July, I went to Berkeley with the wife Yalila to see our son Carl for his Birthday, he is 36 now, plus I saw my Daughter of a previous marriage her name is Annelise and has a PHD in Bioengineering and works at Stanford University in Palo Alto. California.

Had the pleasure to see my Grand Kids Max and Kathya, Max is now 13 and Kathya is 10, I was amazed by Max he plays with Rubik Cube, he arranged it in 9 seconds, the world record is 6 seconds. I posted in Facebook.

Today, July 21, 2016; Trump is given a speech accepting to be nominated for President of the United States, it is

10:33 PM, and I am starting to like him, what is saying to make America great again, he has good plans for America, que talked for one hour and 15 minutes; it the longest speech in the conventions in America, but what he said is what any American that likes this country will agree.

He said he will do better deals with other nations, so America will not be in the deficit side like with China, country that manipulates its money. He also talked about American exceptionalism, which I believe in it. He said he will restore Law and Order, especially just 2 weeks ago 4 policemen were killed, by a resented Army veteran trying to even up, to the idea of Black lives matters, some Policeman were too trigger happy that there was a few Afro Americans killed in d afferent States. But still violence should not be repaid with violence, in my opinion.

In a speech tonight on the third day of the Democratic convention, President Obama said a true statement that is meant against Trump. He said America is great

now, we do not need Trump to make America great, I agree with President Obama, he always says truths that is fact of this country, while Trump exaggerates and says that America is going down and he will make America Great.

Today, I was so disappointed when Trump said on TV the following:" Russia if you are listening I hope you Hack the 30 thousand mails of Hillary Clinton, which is wrong Russia is our adversary as far I know we are in cold war, and Trump admires Vladimir Putin; very strange to admires the person that was a KGB agent before he was President of Russia, plus that was so ridiculous asking Russia just to spite

Hilary Clinton. Very bad experience for me, I was liking Trump but that changed my thoughts.

I was in the US army during the cold war in 1962 to 1964, were I saw missiles on wheels that was programmed to hit Russia, I am sure the Russians have also programed their missiles to hit the west.

Today August 15,2016,I am in Berkeley California,with the purpose to buy a house,so far is going ok, it takes almost a month to finish buying a house, the house I am interested is in Antioch, Ca., a quite area 1 hour and 39 minutes from Berkeley where my Son Carl lives and a Daughter in Palo Alto, my Daughter has a PH in Bio Engineering.

What I am hearing on CNN TV, that Trump is not qualified to be President of the United States, words just said by Joe Biden, vice President of the Unite Stats,
It sounds very insulting,but let is consider is from the Democratic Party, they insult each other just like Trump calls Hillary Clinton, a crooked Lady.

Today is September 7, 2016, I am in Berkeley, Ca At this very moment I am listening the speech of Trump on National Security, his main point he says that America will look for peace through strength. In my opinion is contrary to Obama that believed in Diplomacy which is working now.

I am afraid he might win, he is working that he is better than Hillary Clinton. Trump is acting like he won the elections, It will be a tremendous shock if he loses, he seems positive he will won, he says he will never disappoint the American people, We will see.

Today October 2, 2016 I am in my new home, that my wife and I bought in Antioch, California this is my second week, we drove 2,000 miles all the way from Milwaukee, Wi to Antioch, Ca.

As I sit in my new lovely kitchen I am watching TV, CNN to be exact, where Trump is telling how he did not pay Taxes for 18 years he said he did legally, because he went in bankruptcy I guess for 139 million; but in my opinion seems not fair for a candida to be President, that is not really very honest, while the rest of us will not dare to avoid to pay taxes..

There are like 40 days left before elections, I am almost positive he will win, I know the American people want something different even it is not wise.

Today is October 18, 2016 I moved to Antioch, Ca where my wife and I bought a new house, that is why I stopped a little writing about this elections for President of the USA, but what I find this a very sad situation Trump accuses that this elections are rigged, which I do not believe America has the less corrupt of any nation the world, Mr. Trump is afraid to lose and he probably will blame the media, when he himself a week before the second debate tells in a hidden microphone how he treats women and touch them when he wants, behavior not too good for a candidate,but I am afraid regardless this accusations, the people that like Trump will vote regardless.

Tomorrow is the third and last debate, hope he does not do something that will Hurth him more, right now Hillary Clinton is 47% against 44% for Trump.

President Obama said to Trump stop whining before the game, in three more weeks is the elections.

Today is October 29, 2016, I am really disgusted the way this election is going now 10 days before elections, the FBI is continuing investigating Hillary Clinton about her e mails, a fact the Trump is taking advantage to tell the American people they should not vote for Hillary, but for him that is not corrupt like Hillary; In my opinion he might succeed .Plus he is also playing the Russia card, like Hillary will start the third world war, with the problem of Syria, plus to the point that plying a psychological show to show the world that Russia is preparing for a nuclear exchange; it will not work.

In my case, I voted 3 days ago by mail for the Democratic list, still now Trump might win this election the way I feel.

Surprise today is election Day November 8th,Trump is wining right now it is 10 PM in Antioch, Ca, I am following in MSNBC,Trump is so close to get the 270 electoral votes he is ahead of Hillary Clinton. I am having a coffee.

Trump won the Election on electoral votes, even Hillary won more votes, but the American way they go by delegates of each state, trump added first the necessary votes to be President.

One thing I like that Trump won, is the fact he gets along with Premier Putin of Russia, which is good news, Putin was telling his people we might have a nuclear war, due to the fact Hillary Clinton will ask for no fly zone on Syria, were the Russians fly, that would start a war with Russia, which will not happen now.

Today I am back in Milwaukee for Christmas, to enjoy with my wife, President Elect Trump is coming to West Allis, Wisconsin in the coldest day today is 19 F.

Today President Elect Trump nominated Secretary of State to the CEO of Exon Mobil, Rex Tillerson.

In my opinion, the American senate should go along with Trump nominations, America needs Russia as a friend not as an enemy, considering that Russia has the Atomic capability as the USA, and who needs another Third world where there will be no winners, Earth will be in ruins and they, will not be winners, like the second World Wars, this reminds me what the Scientist Openheimer that formed part of the Manhattan Project that created the Atomic bomb said after the test" I become a destroyer of the world".

Today, December 22 strange word were said both by Trump that nuclear capabilities should be increased, also the same day Putin says pretty much, the same, to me it sounds very bad omen; very bad news I hope Russia and America with Trump we get along, without talking of modernizing, that is like saying we should modernize the way human beings are killed and plus the destruction of the planet.

Today, December 30,2016, after President Obama expelled 35 d Russian Diplomats, to punish Russia for Hacking the Democratic party e mails, to find some dirty stuff against Hillary Clinton, which they find on Podesta a helper of Hillary and some negatives against Hillary.

Today, Putin said he will not retaliate against the USA, instead he invited the children of American diplomats to a New Year Party in the Kremlin. This surprised everybody Trump said he always knew the Putin was Smart.

In my opinion I rather see this, than the beginning f another cold war, I see things will improve with Russia when Trump becomes President on January 20..

Today Jan 4, 2017 Trump gives more creditability to WikiLeaks, than the Russians, what worries me about Trump is he wants to change everything even the way intelligence, a fact no President of the USA will dare to, Trump is unique individual that could be dangerous in the long run.

By warning North Korea that it will not happen for them to develop intercontinental l missile, capable of reaching the USA.

Today in Antioch, Ca is 01/11/17, decide to write after I saw how impolite is President elect Trump to a journalist of CNN, to Acosta a reporter for CNN with 20 years of experience as he said no President of USA was so impolite than Trump. In my 60 years in the USA, never seen that behavior also, but somehow the American people like him and accept for now. His inauguration is in 9 days. The thing that impresses me is he wants to get along with Russia, which is good, we do not want two Atomic armed nations, in cold war again.

Today, January 18th, two days before the inauguration, 60 Democratic Senators will not assist to his inauguration, some are resentful that the Russians assisted Trump, especially Congressman Lewis, a fighter for civil rights close to Luther King.

Anyway, I do not agree with this measure, they have to accept that Trump won the Presidency, and people has or in a Democracy people has to be good losers. Anyway will keep writing about President Trump, my Daughter likes him, me I did not vote for him, but he won. Today January 20th. Trump became the 45th President of the United States; he gave a good speech were he said from now on his government will put America first, well that is what he was saying for a long time; tough some counties like Brazil gave an opinion that mode of thinking might affect Latin America.

Today January 21st they were large marches by women not only in the USA but in different countries, like Mexico, England etc. It is unusual to see so many people to see so many people, before Trump did anything, but unfortunately, they are other people that want change in the USA, I believe this immigration can be the something for years people complain and when a President want to change they can believe, they want to leave the same way it was, but in my opinion, change always comes in the end.

Today January 26th, Trump had an interview last night with ABC Anchor Muir to be exact, in there Trump said he gave the order to build the wall with Mexico, of course Mexico protested but it will be to no avail, Trump is going to do what he promised before the elections, even before the President of Mexico Enrique Peñanieto arrive to the USA on January 31st.

After Trump said in the interview that he will build the wall, in the border with Mexico the President of Mexico canceled his visit, plus Trump said he will tax Mexico in its exports 20% tax.

He did all this in his first week as President, I would say one thing he is a man of his word. Today January 27, trump had his first diplomatic encounter with the Prime Minister of England and tomorrow Saturday he will have a telephone conversation with Putin, President of Russia. Which in my opinion is not a bad idea, I rather be friends with Russia than perpetuate the cold war, I saw on TV yesterday that we are 2 minutes to midnight, meaning and a nuclear war is very close, like during the cold war; we were very close during the Cuban crisis in 1962; they were B29 in their way to Russia and the mission was aborted because Kennedy and Nikita Khrushchev had an agreement, thank God for that.

Today, also President Trump gave an executive order to ban Muslims from 8 or 9 countries, some Iraqi was detained in the JFK airport, it was resolved, the Iraq man wanted to sue the Government, but was resolved amicably., Below some pictures when I was in the US Army, the one with the truck was in Germany.

This is a true Story that the Author Carlos R. Barron, describes in his memoir, after arriving to the USA from Bolivia with a Student Visa, eventually a Professor in the School sponsored him for a green card and was drafted in the USA Army without being a citizen, and the author describes, where he went fun Basic Training, and, Army Radio Repair School, and sent to Germany, to the city of Erlangen where the Armor 4th Division was Stationed, during the cold war in the years 1962 -1964.

Carlos writes about America, his work in the factory and also writes about the last Presidential election and how he sees the Political situation in the 21 first century.

The author lives now in Milwaukee, WI, He is 82 years old and his e mail is barroncertain@gmail.com

About the Author

C arlos R. Barron, a native of Bolivia, came to the United States of America under a student visa. After a professor sponsored him for a green card, he was drafted into the U.S Army. From there, he went to basic training and Army Radio Repair School before being sent to Erlangen, Germany, from 1962-1964, during the Cold War. He currently lives in Milwaukee, Wisconsin.

Printed in the United States
By Bookmasters